Braid Crazy

Simple Steps for Daring 'Dos

by Carla Sinclair

Photographs by Susan Sheridan ✂ Illustrations by Mark Frauenfelder

chronicle books · san francisco

This book is dedicated to my daughter, Sarina.

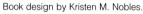

Text © 2003 by Carla Sinclair.
Photographs © 2003 by Susan Sheridan.
Illustrations © 2003 by Mark Frauenfelder.

Book design by Kristen M. Nobles.
Typeset in Helvetica, ITC Century, and Xavier.
The illustrations in this book were rendered in Adobe Illustrator 7.0 for Macintosh.
Manufactured in China.

Library of Congress Cataloging-in-Publication Data
Sinclair, Carla.
Braid crazy : simple steps for daring 'dos / by Carla Sinclair ;
photographs by Susan Sheridan ; illustrations by Mark Frauenfelder.
p. cm.
ISBN 0-8118-3602-9
1. Braids (Hairdressing) I. Frauenfelder, Mark. II. Title.
TT975 .S56 2003
646.7'24—dc21
2002003629

Distributed in Canada by Raincoast Books
9050 Shaughnessy Street, Vancouver, British Columbia V6P 6E5

10 9 8 7 6 5 4 3 2 1

Chronicle Books LLC
85 Second Street, San Francisco, California 94105

www.chroniclekids.com

Contents

Introduction

In elementary school, my friends and I spent lunch hours sitting front to back in a circle, train-style, braiding one another's hair. Nothing fancy—usually just one long braid down the back. But we loved twisting our tresses into shiny, slithering snakes of hair. And of course, this was a chance to catch up on the gossip, like which boy we thought was cute that week.

The combination of hairdos and gossip isn't a new phenomenon. In ancient Egypt, women hosted parties with live music and hairdressers that worked their magic on the party guests. They liked braiding colorful ribbons and lotus flowers into hair, signifying abundance. They also spiced up their braids with precious stones and stained glass. Many Egyptians wore braided wigs (even in the sweltering heat!), which they dyed red, blond, and sometimes even blue.

The ancient Greeks were the first to popularize hair salons, where the Greeks gathered to socialize while they had their braids, cornrows, and twists refreshed.

Braids had a bleak period during the Dark Ages, when hair had to stay close to the head and concealed beneath bonnets or hoods. But braids took a wild turn in the 1600s and 1700s, when hair in France became over-the-top crazy, even absurd, with styles shaped as fruit, boats, even animals, and that reached several feet above the head. Braided hairpieces using up to seven sections, as well as wires, wigs, and small statues, were added to these zany hairdos, or *coiffures*.

Braids have always been a part of hair's history, but thank goodness some things have changed. For instance, today we use hair spray and hair gel to keep our less conspicuous coiffures in place, rather than the beef lard they used to slather on their 'dos. (What a stench!) We also have soft, fuzzy pipe cleaners instead of sharp, scalp-poking wires to help shape our braids when we want something a little crazy, like a set of braided spider legs (see page 58), or a braided pair of pointy cat ears (see page 36).

Braid Crazy goes way beyond the basic braid. The first few pages explain the nuts and bolts—everything you need to know to create all the styles in this book, including techniques, tricks, and accoutrements you may need. Then *Braid Crazy* will take your hair to new and dizzying heights with instructions to make twenty-three unique, ultra-chic braid styles. We start out with easier projects and move on to more complicated styles.

Each braid "recipe" indicates which length of hair works best for that style. "Short" is for girls with hair that ends anywhere from below the ears to right above the shoulders; "medium" is for hair that hangs from the shoulders to the bottom of the shoulder blades. "Long" hair hangs below the shoulder blades. Styles marked "any" work for all three of these lengths. We also have one style—Astro Girl—that works best with "very short" hair, or hair that doesn't make it past the ears. Whether your hair is curly or straight, thick or thin, doesn't make a whit of difference in this book.

Although you'll be able to craft some of these braid styles on your own head of hair, most of them will be a lot easier (and more fun) to do if you find a partner. Get a bunch of friends together and form your own circle-train of hair and chitchat. And remember, the hair recipes in this book are just the beginning. Hair designs are limitless, and even the most novice of braid girls will soon be concocting her own special coiffure. Ready?

Let's go braid crazy!

Braiding Accessories

I keep a lavender plastic toolbox well stocked with the tools and accessories listed here. Three items should always be at hair-length's distance when creating any of the braids in this book:

Spray Bottle—A few squirts of water will tame flyaways and make braiding easier. If you don't have a spray bottle, a cup of water to dunk your brush or comb in will do the trick.

Comb—A great coiffure always requires nice, clean parts, so a comb is a must— preferably a thin one with a long, skinny handle (then you can use the teeth as well as the handle of the comb to part hair).

Large Hair Clips—For many styles you'll need large hair clips—those silver things that kind of look like clothespins that the stylists in beauty salons use—to temporarily clip hair out of the way. If your local drugstore doesn't carry these, you can use "butterfly clips" or something similar, but get the largest ones you can find.

Before you get started with any hairstyle, look at its "Accessories" list and make sure you have all of the necessary tools. Refer to this page if you need help.

Beads—Some braids beg for a flashy array of beads. Look for beads with large openings and lots of sparkling pizzazz. (See page 14 for more on beads.)

Bobby Pins—A must for most hairstyles, even when the recipe doesn't call for them. You never know when you'll need to tame an unruly strand of hair.

Elastics—Elastics are made to hold ponytails without damaging your hair. They come in all colors, and many of them sport funky ornaments, from sparkly balls to shimmery flowers and butterflies. Most of the styles in this book require elastics.

Pipe Cleaners—Used in a handful of styles in this book, pipe cleaners can turn droopy braids into lively spirals, pointy cat ears, and even fuzzy spider legs. I always like to have a variety of colors at my fingertips. (See page 13 for more on braiding with pipe cleaners.)

Ribbons—If you want to turn your braids up a few notches, add some colorful ribbons. Round, cord-like ribbons come in a rainbow of hues and won't twist up as you braid. If you're braiding with a flat ribbon, you'll need to pay attention so that the ribbon doesn't flip over, giving your braid a frumpy, messy look. When a recipe calls for a "strand" of ribbon, the strand should be at least the same length as the hair you are braiding. (See page 13 for more on braiding with ribbons.)

Scrunchies—These decorative, fabric-covered elastics come in handy when you want to hide a hair faux pas, such as the tip of a pipe cleaner poking out of an elastic.

Small Rubber Bands—Although rubber bands can quickly tangle and break hair, very small ones are actually perfect for securing braids at the ends of the hair, where they're less likely to ensnare. You can also use the newer "hair-friendly" plastic bands that come in all colors, as well as clear.

Yarn Needle—Found at craft, fabric, and yarn stores, a yarn needle is helpful when adding ribbon to a ridge braid.

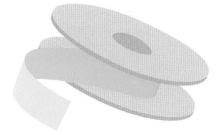

Braiding Techniques

Before you transform your hair into a braided piece of art, make sure you know the drill. Braiding is easy once you get the hang of it, but the fancy finger-work takes a little practice. Quite often you need to use all of your fingers at once—a few to hold the braid in place while the rest are doing other chores (like gathering more hair to add to the braid). There is more than one right way to maneuver your fingers when braiding. The best way to get comfortable is to jump right in and find out what feels best for you. It won't take long—after a few practice runs you'll be off and braiding like a pro.

Simple Braid

Also known as an English braid, the simple braid is the most commonly used braid in this book, and it's the braid we like to use when braiding in ribbons and pipe cleaners. Although it can be made with or without a ponytail, these instructions include the ponytail.

1. Make a ponytail and secure with an elastic.

2. Divide hair from the ponytail into three sections (see illustration 1).

3. Cross the right section over the center section (see illustration 2).

4. Now cross the left section over the center (see illustration 3).

5. Keep alternating sides, crossing the right over the center, then the left over the center, until your braid is complete.

6. Secure the end of the braid with a small rubber band (see illustration 4).

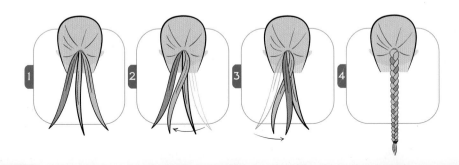

Ridge Braid

Need a braided crown or headband? If so, this is your braid, which wraps *around* the head, rather than moving downward. Although these instructions show you how to move your braid clockwise from the right side of the face, the ridge braid can start anywhere on the head and move in any direction you want.

1. Gather a small handful of hair from the right side of the face and divide into three sections.

2. Begin making a simple braid, crossing the left section over the center, and then the right section over the center.

3. Before crossing the left section over the center again, first gather a small amount of hair (half the size of one of your sections) near the left side of your started braid and add it to your left section. Depending on what type of ridge braid you want, you can either gather the whole depth of the hair (see illustration 1), or you can gather only the top layer so that the braid lies over loose hanging hair (see illustration 2).

4. Cross this thicker left section over the center. Now cross the right section *without* adding new hair.

5. Repeat this process, always adding new hair to the left section before crossing over, but never to the right section.

6. When your ridge braid is as long as you want it you can either secure it with an elastic, letting the long ends hang loosely (see illustration 3), or turn it into a simple braid, securing the end with a small rubber band.

Cornrows

Cornrows require more prep work than other braids, because you need to define the "rows" that make up your pattern before you begin braiding. One of most common cornrow patterns is eight or more parallel braids that run from the forehead to the nape (see Octopus Betty, page 50). If eight rows seems too difficult, try just six or four. They'll be bulkier than traditional cornrows, but you'll still learn the basic technique. You can really do almost anything with this versatile braid, including one long spiral that runs up, down, and all around the head (see Sea Goddess, page 52).

1. Make a center part from forehead to nape. Using a large hair clip, clip one side out of the way.

2. On the unclipped side, make three parallel parts, running from the forehead to the nape, creating four rows of hair. Secure three of the four rows with elastics, leaving one row free to braid (see illustration 1).

3. Gather a small amount of hair nearest the forehead, inside the free row, and divide hair into three sections. Begin making a simple braid, crossing the right section over the center, then the left section over the center (see illustration 2).

4. Add a small amount of hair *from the row you're working on* to the right section (see illustration 3). Cross this thicker section of hair over the center.

5. Add a small amount of hair (again, hair that is inside your defined row) to your left section, and cross this thicker section of hair over the center.

6. Repeat this process until you run out of hair to *add*. If hair is short, secure the end of the cornrow with a small rubber band. If hair is longer, either secure the end of the cornrow with an elastic, letting the remaining hair hang loosely, or turn your cornrow into a simple braid before securing with a small rubber band. (There are other ways to end your cornrow, such as winding remaining hair into buns, or "knots," but let's just stick to the basics here.)

7. Remove the elastic from the next row and repeat steps 3–6 until you have four braids lined up in rows.

8. Now move to the other side of the head and repeat steps 2–7 until all eight of your cornrows are secured (see illustration 4).

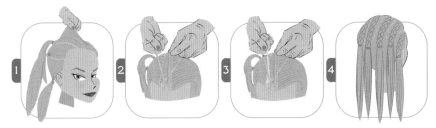

Flat Twist

Similar to a cornrow, the flat twist is a nice, quick alternative. Instead of three sections of hair you need only two sections to make this "braid."

1. Prepare rows as you do for cornrows (see Cornrows steps 1–2).

2. Gather a small amount of hair nearest the forehead, inside the free row, and divide the hair into only two sections. Cross the left section over the right (see illustration 1).

3. Add a small amount of hair from within your row, closest to your twist, to each section (see illustration 2), and then, again, cross the left section over the right.

4. Keep adding hair to each section, then crossing the left section over the right, until you reach the end of your row.

5. Secure with an elastic (see illustration 3).

6. Remove the elastic from the next row and repeat steps 2–5 until you have four flat twists lined up in rows.

7. Now move to the other side of the head and repeat steps 2–6 until all eight of your flat twists are secured.

Hairline Twist

Although not really a braid, making a hairline twist is a skill all braiders should have in their repertoire.

1. Gather a small amount of hair at the top of your hairline (near your forehead) and twist a couple of times, making sure to hold the hair up and back while twisting.

2. Moving along the hairline toward your nape, take another thin section of hair and add it to your twist, twisting once again (see illustration).

3. Repeat until your hairline twist is at the length you want.

4. Either secure with an elastic or a barrette, or do like Dorothy did and turn it into a braid (see page 18).

Fishtail

A great substitute for the simple braid, the fishtail is perfect for those who want a unique and more intricate-looking style (although it's a cinch to do). For a sleeker fishtail, pull tightly as you braid.

1. Make a ponytail, secure with an elastic, and divide the hair into two sections (see illustration 1).

2. Take a thin strand of hair from the back of the right section and cross it over to the front of the left section (see illustration 2).

3. Take a thin strand of hair from the back of the left section and cross it over to the front of the right section (see illustration 3).

4. Continue this process until your fishtail is complete. Secure it with an elastic or small rubber band (see illustration 4).

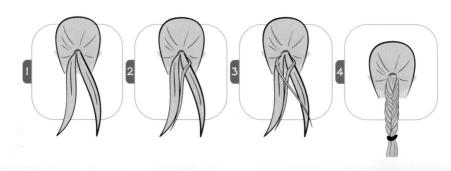

Braided Coil

Depending on the style, coils can add more funk or elegance to your braided 'do. A coil usually needs 2–4 bobby pins to keep it secured.

1. Make a ponytail, secure with an elastic, and make a simple braid, securing the end with a small rubber band.

2. Wind the braid around its elastic base (see illustration).

3. After the braid is completely wound, tuck the end under the coil and secure with bobby pins.

Braiding in Ribbons or Pipe Cleaners

This technique works best with simple braids that begin as a ponytail. Use up to three ribbons or pipe cleaners per braid.

1. Make a ponytail and secure with an elastic.

2. Slip the ends of the ribbons or pipe cleaners underneath the elastic and bend the tips of pipe cleaners down, so that each pipe cleaner is secured and hangs down with the rest of the hair (see illustration 1).

3. Divide the ponytail into three sections, and lay the ribbon strands or pipe cleaners over the sections—one ribbon or pipe cleaner per section. When using fewer than three ribbons or pipe cleaners, one or two sections of hair will be unadorned. Keep the ribbon or pipe cleaner on top as you braid, rather than letting it get lost within the hair (see illustration 2). On a thin braid, use just one strand of ribbon or one pipe cleaner, to act as one of the braid's three sections (see illustration 3).

4. Secure the braid with a small rubber band and trim your ribbon strands or pipe cleaners if they're too long (see illustration 4).

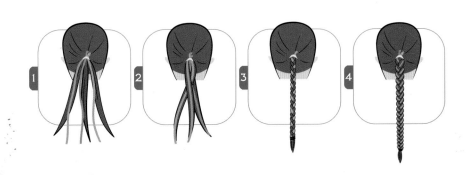

Weaving in Ribbons

When working with a French or ridge braid, it's easier to *weave* in ribbons.

1. Thread a yarn needle with ribbon (see page 7 for more on yarn needles).

2. Sew the ribbon into a finished braid, weaving under and over the sections as you move toward the end of the braid (see illustration). You may want to add two strands per ridge braid, for extra pizzazz.

Adding Beads

If braids are extra thin, simply slip a bead over each braid, as high up on the braid as desired. If beads hang on the end of the braids, secure a small rubber band underneath the beads so that they don't slip off.

Beads can be added to thicker braids that start off as ponytails by first stringing the beads onto thread. To prevent the beads from sliding around on the thread, after each bead is strung, wrap the thread up to the top of the bead and knot it, then slip the remaining thread back down through the bead's opening.

Once the thread is beaded, adding it to a braid is like braiding with ribbons (see above). Slip the tip of the thread underneath the ponytail's elastic, or tie the thread around the elastic and knot it. Divide the hair into three sections, laying the string of beads neatly over one of the sections. Always keep the beads on top of the hair as you braid, so that they will show.

The 'Dos

Now that you've mastered the basics, it's time to get started. Check out the hair length chart below to find a style that's just right for you.

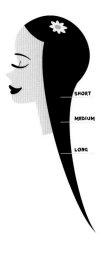

Pippi Longstocking

For the girl who wants the most shock value out of her braids, this gravity-defying style will do the trick. It works best on thinner hair, and unless you've got extra-long pipe cleaners, hair should hover somewhere around the shoulders.

1. Make a center part from forehead to nape.

2. Make two high ponytails, one on either side of the head, and secure with the elastics.

3. Slip three pipe cleaners into each elastic and bend the tips down so that each pipe cleaner is secured and hangs down with the rest of the hair (see illustration 1).

4. Place the small scrunchies or wide ribbon over the elastics to hide the bent pipe cleaner tips.

5. Divide one ponytail into three sections, making sure one pipe cleaner lies neatly over each section, and braid. Secure the end with a small rubber band (see illustration 2). If desired, cover the small rubber band with a small scrunchie.

6. Repeat step 5 on the other ponytail.

7. If pipe cleaners extend beyond the braid ends, snip them to size.

8. Now the fun part. Curve each braid upward, as if they're reaching for the moon. Step outside and see your neighbors' reactions.

Accessories

2 elastics

6 pipe cleaners

4 small scrunchies or strands of wide ribbon

2 small rubber bands

Techniques

Simple braid

Braiding in pipe cleaners

Hair length

Medium

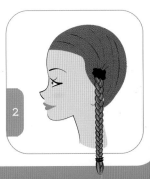

Dorothy

It's easy to confuse Dorothy braids with two simple pigtail braids. But watch *The Wizard of Oz* closely and see that a true Dorothy braid has a few extra steps that give it that original Kansas-girl look.

1. Make a center part from forehead to nape. Use the large hair clip to clip the left side away.

2. On the right side, begin making a hairline twist.

3. Twist along the hairline, stopping just near the top of the ear. Give the hair one more firm twist, and while holding on to that twist, divide the remaining loose hair into two equal sections (see illustration).

4. Begin a simple braid, using the loose hair from the twist as the third section.

5. Stop the braiding midway down the length of the hair and secure with an elastic.

6. Unclip the left side and repeat steps 1–4.

7. Tie the blue ribbon over the elastics and click your heels together three times.

Accessories

1 large hair clip
2 elastics
2 strands of blue ribbon

Techniques

Hairline twist
Simple braid

Hair length

Medium–long

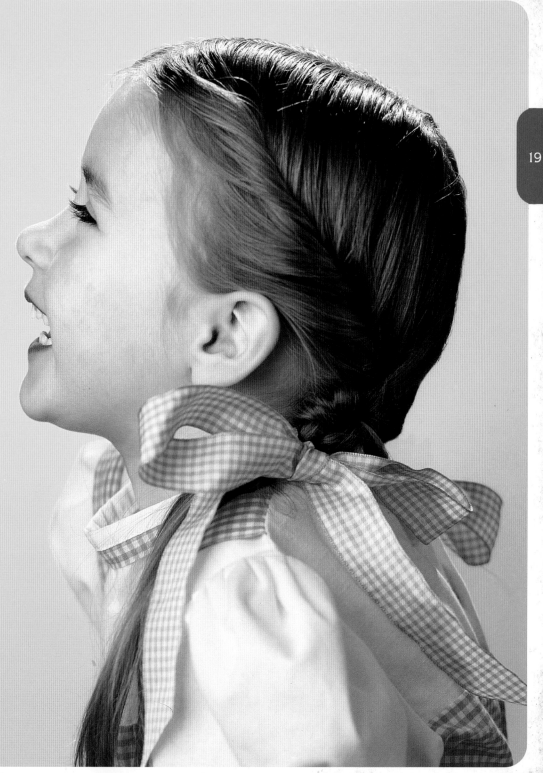

Miss Muffet

OK, so we're cheating a little. You won't find a true braid in this style, but we find it worthy for its good ol' storybook charm. If you're a real stickler, however, just braid rather than twist.

1. Make a center part from forehead to nape.

2. Make two ponytails, one on either side of the head, and secure with the elastics.

3. Take one ponytail and twist, twist, twist (see illustration 1).

4. Coil the twisted ponytail around the elastic (see illustration 2), then secure the spiral bun with bobby pins. If your hair is long, you may have to keep alternating so that you twist, coil, secure with a bobby pin; twist, coil, secure with a bobby pin… until you work your way to the end of the ponytail.

5. Repeat on the other side. If you spot a spider in the process, simply move to another tuffet and try again.

Accessories

2 elastics
Bobby pins

Techniques

Coil

Hair length

Medium–long

Heidi

Here's an updo that works just as well for a school graduation as it does for a picnic in the Alps. They're perfect braids to decorate with wildflowers before belting out your favorite yodels.

1. Make a center part from forehead to nape. Use the large hair clip to clip the left side out of the way.

2. On the right side, braid the hair and secure the end with a small rubber band.

3. Unclip the left side and repeat step 2.

4. Lift one of the braids up and wrap it over the top of the head, toward the opposite ear. You can position the braid so that it lies across the middle of the crown, or closer to the top of your forehead.

5. Fold the end of the braid underneath itself (see illustration) and secure the braid to the head with bobby pins. Unless you're using fancy pins, try securing them underneath the braid so that they don't show.

6. Lift the second braid and cross it over the first. Fold the end of the braid under and secure with bobby pins.

7. Liven up your Heidi braids by attaching decorative clips or faux flowers.

Accessories

1 large hair clip

2 small rubber bands

Bobby pins

Decorative hair clips or small faux flowers

Techniques

Simple braid

Hair length

Long

Hula Dancer

Accessories

1 elastic
6 strands of ribbon
6 small rubber bands
Bobby pins

Techniques

Simple braid
Braiding in ribbons
Braided coil

Hair length

Any

Fresh flowers usually lose their zest or completely vanish within minutes of pinning them to your hair. But not so with a braided flower, which never wilts and never disappears. Swipe your ribbon with a bit of gardenia or jasmine oil before braiding for some aromatic luau oomph.

1. Gather a handful of hair from one side of the natural part and make a ponytail. Secure with the elastic.

2. Slip the six strands of ribbon underneath the elastic and, using all of the hair from the ponytail, make six thin braids. Use one strand of ribbon as the third section of each braid. Secure the ends with the small rubber bands (see illustration 1).

3. While holding the braids together, coil them (see illustration 2).

4. Secure the braided "flower" with bobby pins. Aloha!

Jean Genie

Accessories

2 elastics (1 regular and 1 decorative elastic)

1 strand of thick, cord-like ribbon

2 small rubber bands

Bobby pins

3 strands of ribbon

Techniques

Simple braid

Braiding in ribbons

Hair length

Medium–long

This style looks a lot more mysterious than it really is. In fact, it takes only five minutes to do. Just make sure that your fancy elastic has a jewel-like bauble attached to it—we like bright gems or glittery plastic balls—to give it that extra dreamy flair.

1. Starting on one side of the head, part hair from ear to ear.

2. Pull the front half of the hair into a low ponytail in front of the face and secure with the decorative elastic. Make sure the ornament on the elastic is underneath the pony-tail (see illustration 1).

3. Slip the thick, cord-like ribbon underneath the elastic and braid the ponytail, dividing the hair into two sections and using the ribbon as the third section. Secure the end with a small rubber band.

4. Wind the braid up, then pull the wound braid tautly behind the elastic, so that it sits on top of the head, and secure it with bobby pins (see illustration 2).

5. If desired, pull all loose hair into a ponytail at the back of the head and secure with an elastic. Slip two strands of ribbon underneath the elastic and braid the ponytail, making sure each ribbon lies neatly on top of each section. Secure the end with a rubber band. To hide the elastic and small rubber band, tie some ribbon around them. Magic-carpet time!

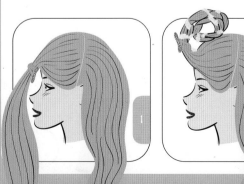

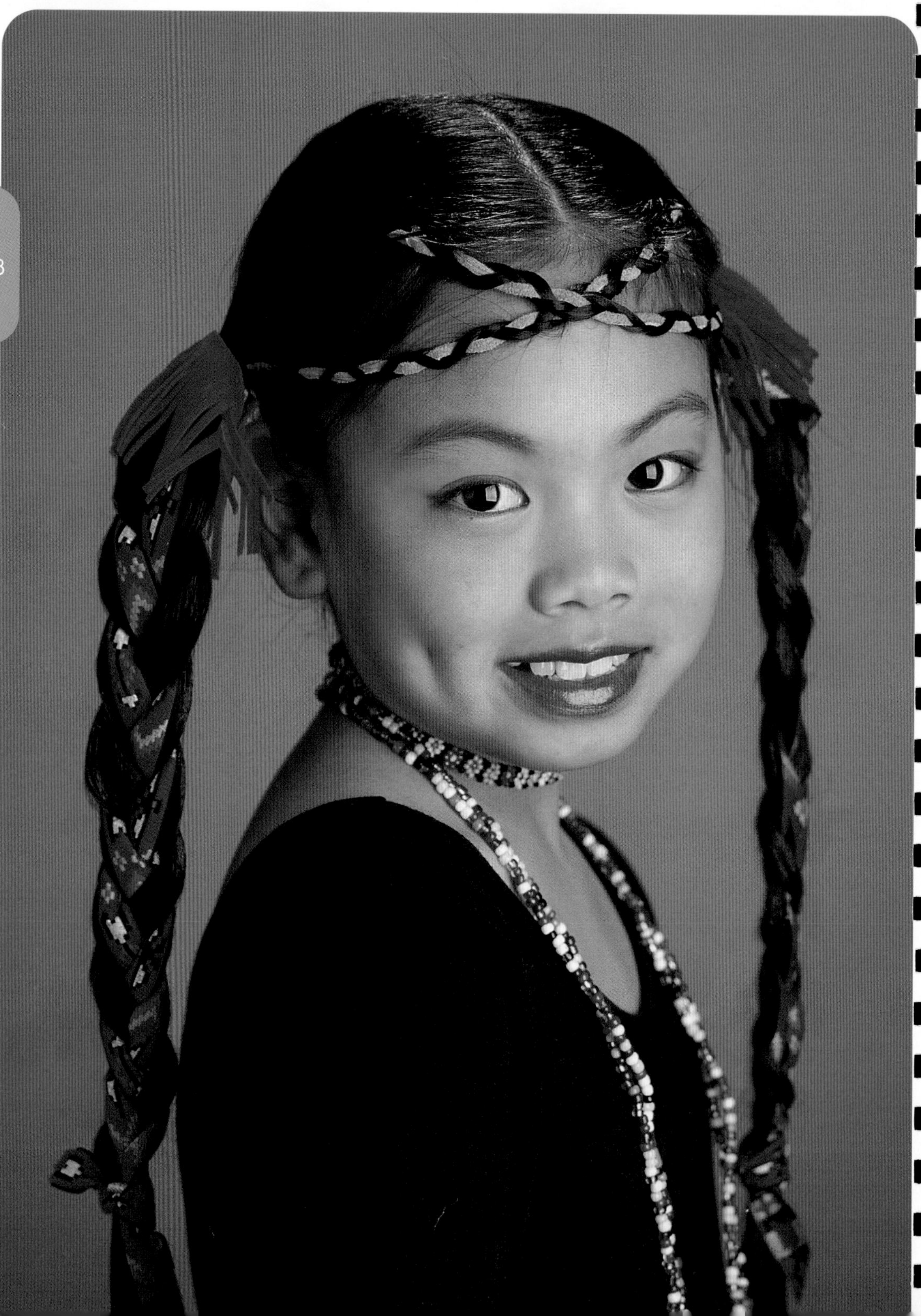

Pocahontas

Although this style looks great straight from the recipe, feel free to add your own ingredients: feathers, beads, and colorful clip-on braids (found at most beauty supply shops).

1. Make a center part from forehead to nape.

2. Gather enough hair to make two small ponytails on either side of the face, and secure each by knotting a strand of ribbon around the top of the to-be-braided hair. Divide each ponytail into two sections and braid, using the ribbon as the third section.

3. Instead of using small rubber bands, secure the ends with the hair clips.

4. Drape the left braid across the forehead to the right side. Holding this braid in your right hand, use your left hand to gather it and the rest of the hair on the right side of the head into a ponytail. Secure with an elastic (see illustration). If the braid tightens up on the forehead, *gently* loosen it from the ponytail until it drapes the way you want it to.

5. Repeat step 4 on the other side of the head.

6. Unclip both braids and unravel them up to the elastics. Trim ribbons so that they hang just below each elastic.

7. Slip two new strands of ribbon under each elastic, making sure not to let the ribbon from the thinner braids slip out. Cover the elastics and ribbon tips with scrunchies.

8. Braid the ponytails, making sure each ribbon lies neatly on top of each section. One section of hair will be unadorned. Secure the ends with the small rubber bands, and if there is any remaining ribbon, tie it around the small rubber bands.

Accessories

6 strands of ribbon
2 large hair clips
2 elastics
2 scrunchies
2 small rubber bands

Techniques

Simple braid
Braiding in ribbons

Hair length

Medium–long

Bahama Mama

This quickie will add an exotic, tropical touch to any outfit. Although we recommend long hair, medium–long hair will work as well. But you'll need to ease up on the winding (you might only get one round in), and you'll have to settle for a braided kiwi fruit, rather than a majestic pineapple coiffure.

1. Gather hair into a high ponytail on top of the head and secure with the elastic.

2. Slip the ribbon underneath the elastic and braid the ponytail, dividing the hair into two sections and using the ribbon as the third section. Stop braiding three inches before the end of the hair and secure with the small rubber band. Trim the ribbon just below the small rubber band.

3. Coil the braid into a pineapple-shaped mound, stacking the braid as you coil to give it height. Slip the end under the base of the mound from the back (see illustration), and pull it up through the top.

4. Secure the mound with bobby pins. If you have loose ribbon ends, you can tie them around the top of the mound or trim them to match hair ends.

5. Fan out the hair ends and spritz lightly with hair spray.

Accessories

1 elastic
1 strand of wide ribbon
1 small rubber band
Bobby pins

Techniques

Simple braid
Braiding in ribbons
Braided coil

Hair length

Long

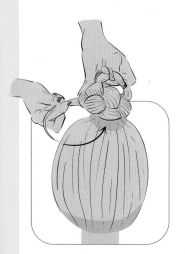

Frida Kahlo

Accessories

2 elastics

6 strands of thin ribbon
(double length of hair)

2 strands of wide ribbon
(double length of hair)

2 small rubber bands

Bobby pins

Faux flowers

Techniques

Simple braid

Braiding in ribbons

Hair length

Long

As we see it, art is created through many
mediums, hair included. *¡Qué bonita!*

1. Make a center part from forehead to nape.

2. Using all the hair, make two ponytails, one on either
side of the head, and secure with the elastics.

3. Slip three strands of thin ribbon underneath each elastic.
The ribbons should hang eight inches longer than the hair.

4. Take one strand of wide ribbon and tie its end around the
elastic on one side of the head. The rest of the ribbon should
hang eight inches longer than the hair. With the other strand
of wide ribbon, repeat on the other side (see illustration 1).

5. Braid each ponytail by dividing the hair into two sections, using the wide ribbon as the third section. Lay all
three strands of thin ribbon neatly over one section of hair,
leaving the second section of hair unadorned. Secure the
end of each braid—which should have four long strands
of ribbon sticking out—with a small rubber band.

6. Lift both braids up toward the front, top center of the
head and wrap the braids around each other once (see
illustration 2) to create a small "knob" on top of the head.

7. While holding the knob to keep the braids in place,
bring the end of each braid back down to its original side,
wrapping it around the root of the
braid a few times. Secure each
braid to the head with bobby pins.
Arrange ribbons so that they
frame the face. Finish by slipping
faux flowers into the braids and
securing with bobby pins.

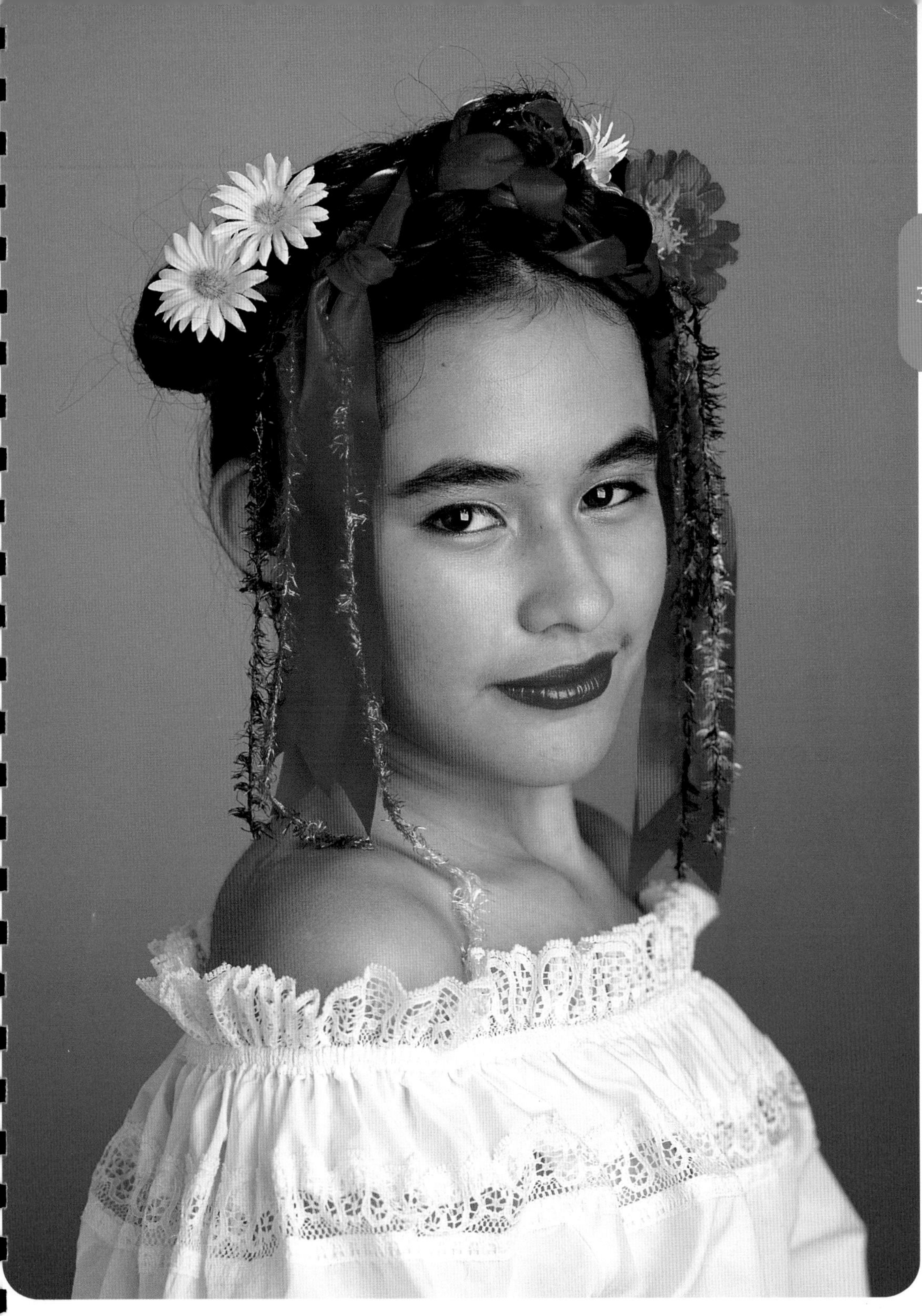

Hippie Chick

Got a pair of worn jeans and a tie-dyed peasant top? Add this colorful braided headband.

1. Make a center part from forehead to nape.

2. Make a ridge braid, starting at the back of the head, just right of the part, and working clockwise. Use only the top layer of hair, so that the braid lies over loose hanging hair (see illustration 1). Since this will be a braided "headband," position the braid so that it runs around the side of the head, just above the ear.

3. When you reach the forehead, switch to a simple braid. Make this part of the braid long enough to lie across the center of the forehead, headband-style (see illustration 2).

4. Revert back to a ridge braid once you get to the other side of the face (see illustration 3).

5. When your braid has come full circle, which should be at the back of the head, you will have leftover hair from your ridge braid. Braid this and secure it with a small rubber band.

6. Let the simple braid hang down, or tuck it into the top of the ridge braid and secure with bobby pins.

7. Make at least four very thin braids with the loose hair that frames the face and add some beads to them. Secure with small rubber bands.

Accessories

5 small rubber bands
Bobby pins
Beads

Techniques

Ridge braid
Simple braid
Adding beads

Hair length

Medium–long

Catty Grrrl

Whether you're headed for a costume party or just feeling silky sleek, what could be more purr-fect than a pair of pointy cat ears? This style will surely bring the feline out in you.

1. Make a center part from forehead to nape.

2. Make two small ponytails on top of the head, adjacent to the forehead and the center part, and secure with small rubber bands.

3. Slip one pipe cleaner underneath each rubber band and bend the tips down so that each pipe cleaner is secured (see illustration 1).

4. Braid each ponytail, dividing the hair into two sections and using the pipe cleaner as the third section. Secure the ends with the small rubber bands. Trim the pipe cleaners to size.

5. Crease each braid two inches from the rubber band, creating a pointy cat ear. Wrap the rest of the braid around the base of the cat ear (see illustration 2), tuck the end underneath the braid, and secure with bobby pins. Hiss! A catty grrrl you are.

On second thought: You don't think of yourself as the catty type? Just add a pretty red bow to the base of the left cat ear, look in the mirror, and say, "Hello, Kitty!"

Accessories

4 small rubber bands
2 pipe cleaners
Bobby pins

Techniques

Simple braid
Braiding in pipe cleaners

Hair length

Any

Snow Bunny

Unlike your typical heavy-duty winter wear, these braided earmuffs are the kind you can wear all year round. Now, if only we could come up with some braided mittens to match.

1. Make a center part from forehead to nape.

2. Make a very small ponytail above the ear on either side of the head and secure by knotting a strand of ribbon or yarn around the top of the to-be-braided hair. Divide each ponytail into two sections and braid, using the ribbon or yarn as the third section.

3. Instead of using small rubber bands, secure the ends with the large hair clips (see illustration 1).

4. Take each braid and cross it over to the other side of the head so that the braids lie parallel to each other on top of the head.

5. Using the rest of the hair, make two high ponytails, one on each side of the head. Unclip the braids and include them in the ponytails. Secure with the elastics.

6. Unravel both braids up to the elastics. Trim the ribbons two inches below the elastics (see illustration 2).

7. Slip up to three strands of ribbon or yarn underneath each elastic, making sure not to let the ribbon from the thin braids slip out.

8. Braid the ponytails, making sure each ribbon lies neatly on top of each section. Secure the ends with the small rubber bands.

9. Coil each braid and secure with bobby pins.

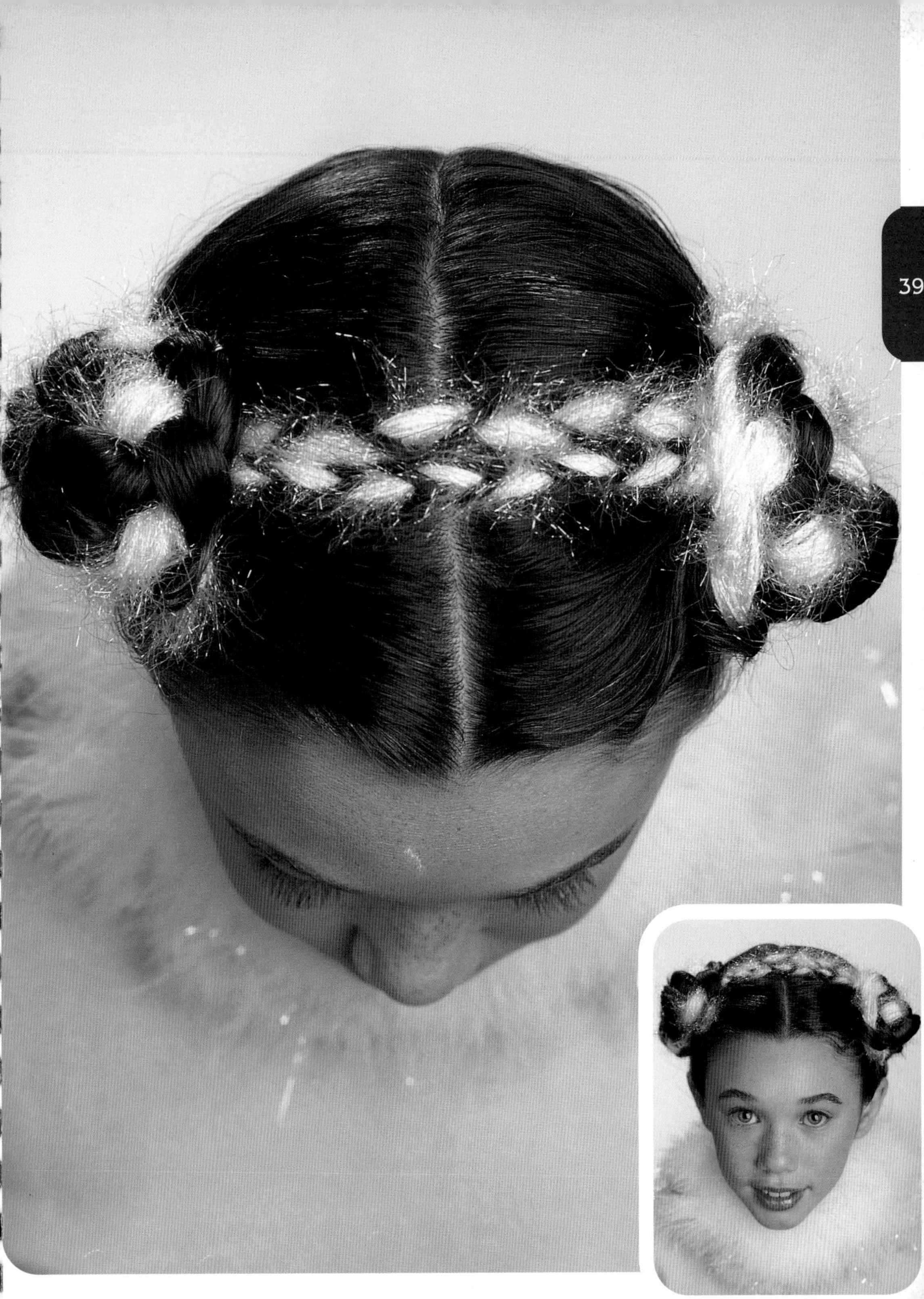

Pirate Matey

Pirates aren't always greasy, grimy slobs with stubble on their faces. A Pirate Matey is as sparkly as a stash of newfound jewels.

1. Make a center part from forehead to nape.

2. Make six small ponytails that frame the face—four on the left side of the part and two on the right—and secure with small rubber bands.

3. Slip a strand of ribbon under each rubber band, and braid each ponytail by dividing it into two sections, using the ribbon as the third section (see illustration 1). Secure the end of each braid with a large hair clip.

4. Once all of your braids are completed, unclip them and pull them into a ponytail with the rest of your hair above and behind the right ear. Secure with the elastic (see illustration 2).

5. Unravel the braids up to the elastic, and trim the ribbons two inches below the elastic.

6. Slip six new strands of ribbon under the elastic, making sure not to let the ribbon from the small braids slip out.

7. Using all of the hair in the ponytail, make two braids, with three strands of ribbon per braid. Make sure the ribbon lies neatly on top of each section as you braid. Secure with small rubber bands. You should have six braids above the elastic, and two braids below it. Slip the scrunchie over the elastic. Ships ahoy!

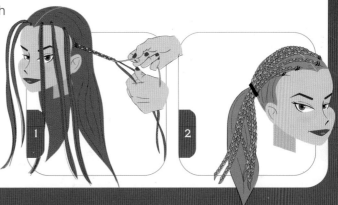

Accessories

8 small rubber bands

12 strands of ribbon

6 large hair clips

1 elastic

1 scrunchie

Techniques

Simple braid

Braiding in ribbons

Hair length

Medium–long

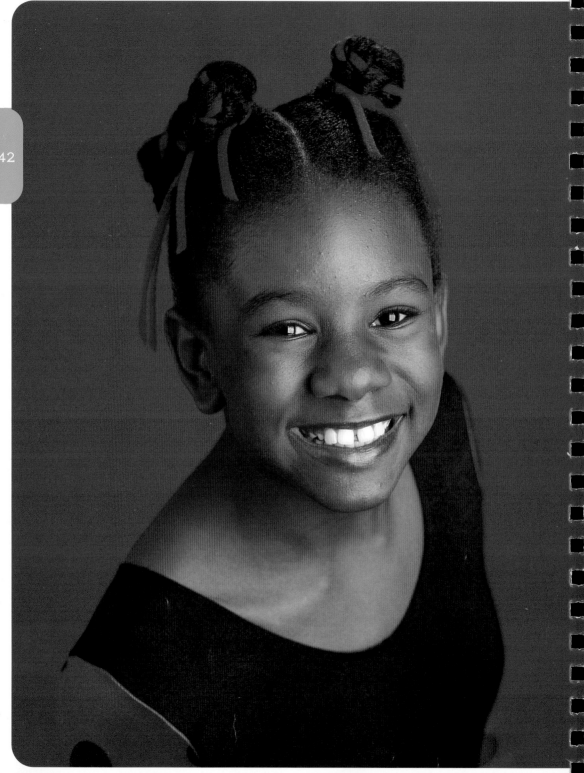

Lady Bug

Although this hairdo goes great with dressing up, we also like wearing it without ribbon on the beach and on hiking days to keep hair off our shoulders and in one place. For an added bonus, unravel your braided "spots" at the end of the day and enjoy your new wild waves.

1. Make a center part from forehead to nape.

2. Using all of the hair, make six ponytails on top and around the head and secure with the elastics.

3. Slip one double-length strand of ribbon underneath each elastic and pull until there are two equal lengths of ribbon that hang down with—and three inches past—each ponytail. Braid each ponytail, making sure each ribbon lies neatly on top of each section. Since there are only two strands of ribbon, one section of the braid will be unadorned. Secure the ends with the small rubber bands.

4. Coil each braid, making sure the side with the ribbon is facing outward. Tuck the end of each braid under the coil and secure with bobby pins.

5. Arrange the dangling "legs" of the ribbon so that they hang in front of each coil.

Accessories

6 elastics

6 strands of double length (plus six inches) black or red ribbon

6 small rubber bands

Bobby pins

Techniques

Simple braid

Braiding in ribbons

Braided coil

Hair length

Any

Saturn de Milo

The planet Saturn may be as old as the universe, but this orbiting 'do is for the ultra *moderne.* Fit for any chic party, formal outing, or intergalactic occasion.

1. Make a center part from forehead to nape.

2. Gather a handful of hair on top of the head and pull it into a ponytail, securing it with the elastic. Leave about an inch of loose hair between the forehead and the ponytail (see illustration 1).

3. Slip the three strands of ribbon underneath the elastic and braid the ponytail, making sure each ribbon lies neatly on top of each section. Secure the end with the small rubber band.

4. Coil your braid and secure with bobby pins.

5. Starting from the back of the head and using the rest of the hair, make a ridge braid that circles your braided "planet" (see illustration 2).

6. Once you've come full circle, finish by making a simple braid with the remaining hair and tuck it along the top inside of the ridge braid. Secure with bobby pins.

7. For a more vibrant Saturn-style ring, add shiny hair jewels to the ridge braid, or use a yarn needle to weave some electric ribbon into it.

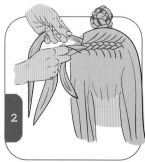

Accessories

1 elastic

3 strands of ribbon

1 small rubber band

Bobby pins

Optional: hair jewels or ribbon and yarn needle

Techniques

Simple braid

Braiding in ribbons

Braided coil

Ridge braid

Hair length

Medium–long

Astro Girl

Short-haired girls rule when it comes to this asteroid-kicking style. Although we piped in radiant rocket-fire colors, using black pipe cleaners or creating a pattern with colors also rocks. And now for the countdown…

1. Using all of the hair, make about twenty small ponytails all over the head and secure with small rubber bands.

2. Slip one pipe cleaner underneath one of the small rubber bands, then divide the ponytail into two sections and use the pipe cleaner as the third section to make a braid.

3. Secure the braid with a small rubber band, then trim the pipe cleaner to size.

4. Take the pencil and tightly wrap the braid around it. Then slip the pencil out, and you'll have a springy coil.

5. Repeat steps 2–4 until every ponytail is transformed into a bright, spiraling antenna. Ready for blastoff!

Accessories

Approximately 40 small rubber bands

Approximately 20 pipe cleaners

Pencil (preferably unsharpened)

Techniques

Simple braid

Braiding in pipe cleaners

Hair length

Very short–short

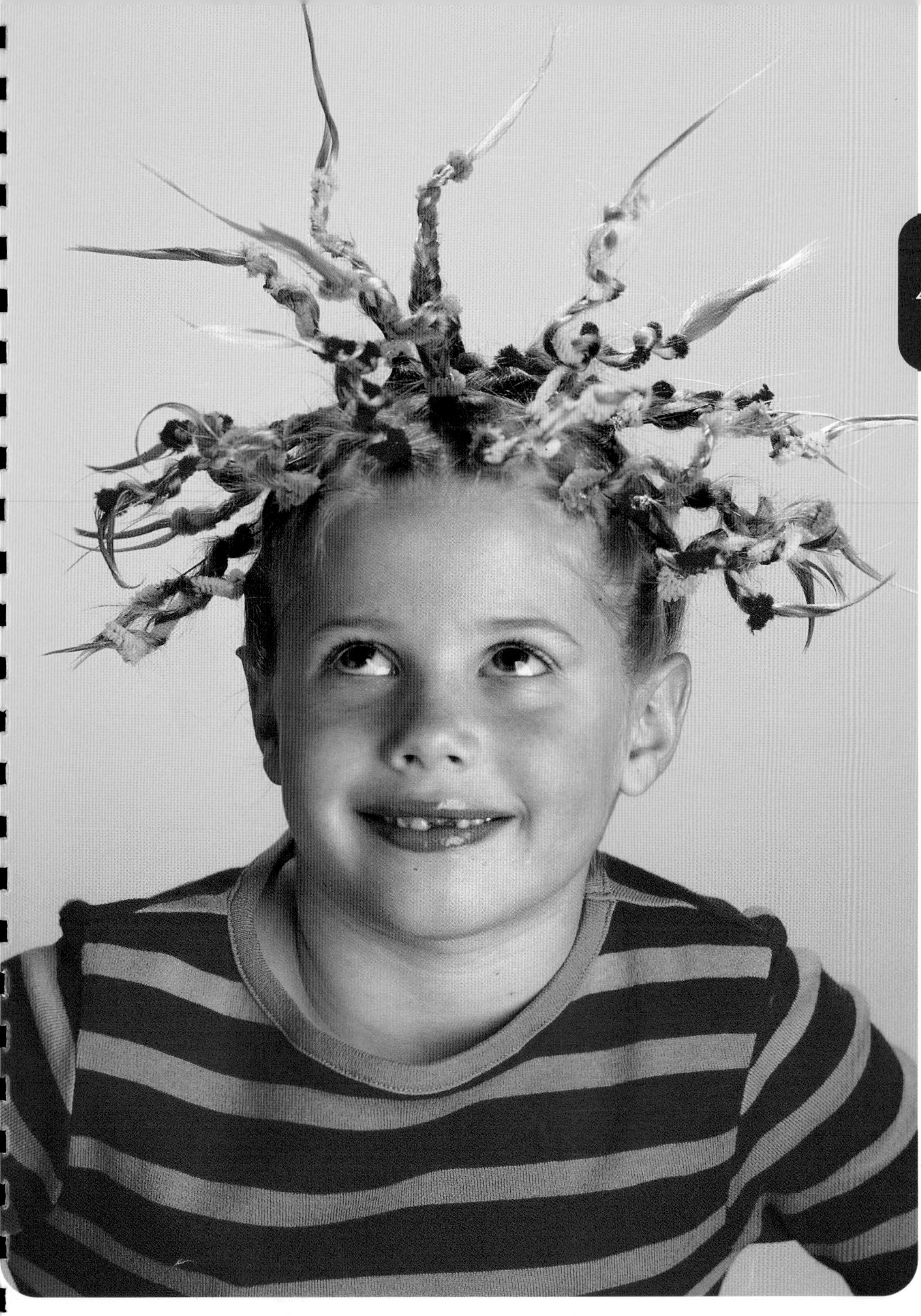

Crowned Princess

One of the most elegant braids in this book, Crowned Princess is great for dressing up. For a less royal look, you can also make a braided crown with nothing but a small rubber band and a few bobby pins, which makes this one of those styles you can do anywhere, anytime.

1. Make a center part from forehead to nape.

2. Using all of the hair, make a ridge braid, starting at the back of the head, moving clockwise. Unlike other ridge braids in this book, position this one so that it lies on *top* of the head, like a crown (see illustration). If hair is too short to add the underneath layers, add only the top layer, letting the underneath layers hang loose.

3. When you reach the top of the forehead, switch to a simple braid. Make this long enough to run along the front top of the head, then revert back to the ridge braid until you've gone full circle.

4. Once you've completed your crown, make a simple braid with any leftover hair, secure it with the small rubber band, and tuck it along the inside top of the ridge braid. Secure with bobby pins.

5. Use the yarn needle to weave the ribbon into the braid, and a royal crown it shall be.

On second thought: If, at the last minute, you decide to change your status from single to hitched, a Princess Bride you can be. Just weave in a white ribbon, then attach some white faux or fresh flowers around your braided crown.

Accessories

1 small rubber band
Bobby pins
Yarn needle
1 strand of colorful ribbon

Techniques

Ridge braid
Simple braid
Weaving in ribbon

Hair length

Any

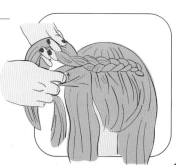

Octopus Betty

Accessories

8 elastics with ocean-colored plastic balls or funky baubles

8 small rubber bands

8 strands of ocean-colored ribbon

Techniques

Cornrows

Fishtail or simple braid

Hair length

Any

Although this coiffure takes a small chunk of time to do, it has a lot of things going for it: (1) it looks awesome, (2) it's a hair-friendly style for swimmers that doesn't tangle or get in your face, and (3) if braided with care, you can leave it in for weeks. Just remember to gently shampoo your scalp every few days.

1. Make a center part from forehead to nape.

2. Using all of the hair, make eight parallel cornrows from the forehead to the nape. When you reach the nape, secure each cornrow with a decorative elastic (see illustration).

3. With the remaining loose hair from each cornrow, make a fishtail and secure the ends with a small rubber band. If hair is short, make a simple braid rather than a fishtail and secure with a small rubber band.

4. Tie a strand of ribbon over each small rubber band and trim the ribbon three inches from the end of the braid, so that it dangles like cool, shimmery seaweed.

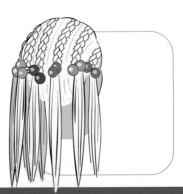

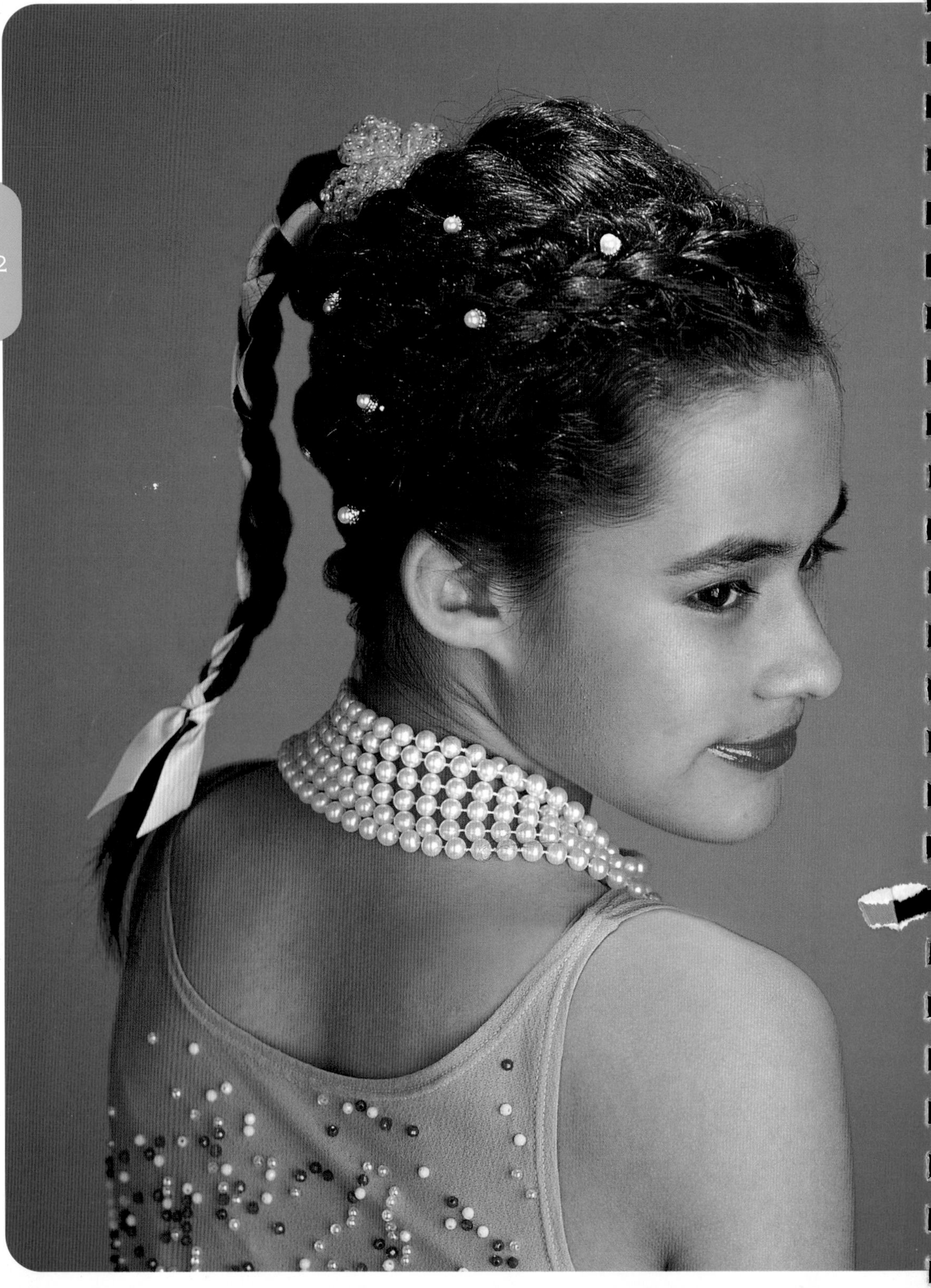

Sea Goddess

This spiraling cornrow takes a circular path around and around the head, making it one of our more adventurous styles. The goddess-to-be may have to help out by bending way forward or to the side, but she'll be rewarded with an awesome, sparkling, shell-shaped 'do.

1. Prepare a cornrow by making a part that starts at the top of the forehead and runs down the far right side of the head. Use a large hair clip to clip aside hair that isn't in the row.

2. Make the cornrow (see illustration 1). When you reach the nape, use the other large hair clip to clip the braid so that it doesn't unravel.

3. Prepare to change the direction of the cornrow by making a new part that runs horizontally, along the bottom of the scalp from right to left. Use the first clip to clip aside hair that isn't in the new row.

4. Unclip the braid and continue the cornrow in its new left-bound direction. Since the braid is now "sideways," your sea goddess may want to tilt her head down to her left to make braiding as easy as possible.

Accessories

2 large hair clips

1 fancy elastic

1 strand of ribbon

1 small rubber band

Clip-on pearls or jewels

Techniques

Cornrows

Simple braid

Hair length

Any

Sea Goddess

5. Ready for a challenge? Clip the braid again and make a new part that runs back *up* the left side of the head (see illustration 2). Braiding upward feels weird at first, especially for the sea goddess, who may want to tilt her head sideways and forward. (Does this count as a yoga pose?)

6. Once you've braided up to the left side of the head, make a part toward the right, back to where you started.

7. Once you come full circle, stop and plan to braid downward again, this time on the inside of your first downward cornrow.

8. Continue parting and extending the cornrow in a spiraling clockwise direction until the braid ends up in the center of the scalp and has nowhere else to go.

9. Make a ponytail with the remaining hair and secure with the fancy elastic. Slip the ribbon underneath the elastic and make a braid, dividing the hair into two sections and using the ribbon as the third section. Secure with the small rubber band, and tie any remaining ribbon around the small rubber band.

10. Finally, do what every sea goddess does and clip on some pearls or other sea-like jewels to decorate the braid.

Guinevere

Hear ye m'ladies! 'Tis only eight steps, and ye shall be granted the loveliest of medieval maiden tresses. Make sure to have thy large hair clips handy for this one.

1. Gathering only the top layer of hair, make six small ponytails, evenly spaced around the top of the head, and secure with small rubber bands. The two ponytails closest to the face should be half the thickness of the other four.

2. Slip one strand of ribbon underneath each small rubber band that is closest to the face, and secure two strands of ribbon underneath each of the other four rubber bands. The ribbons can all be the same color, but don't be afraid to mix and match.

3. Starting with the first ponytail on the right side of the head, make a braid by dividing the hair into two sections, using the ribbon as the third section. Braid only halfway down, and when the ribbon is the section that is closest to the next ponytail, use a large hair clip to clip the partial braid out of the way (see illustration 1).

4. Working clockwise around the head, divide the next ponytail into two sections and use the other large hair clip to clip the left section out of the way.

Accessories

11 small rubber bands
12 strands of thin ribbon
2 large hair clips

Techniques

Simple braid
Braiding in ribbons

Hair length

Any

Guinevere

5. With the right section, make a braid by dividing the hair into two sections, using the ribbon as the third section. When the braid is halfway down, and when the ribbon is the section that is closest to the first braid, hold on to the second braid while carefully unclipping the first, making sure not to let either braid unravel.

6. Merge both braids into one. To do this, carefully separate each strand of ribbon from its braid and put them together. The two strands of ribbon make up one section of hair, while the two sections of hair from each braid join together to become one section each (see illustration 2). Braid down to the ends and secure with a small rubber band.

7. Unclip the left section of the second ponytail and repeat step 5.

8. Continue working around the head, repeating steps 3–6 until you've gone full circle.

9. To top off your lovely locks, cut the last two strands of ribbon into pieces big enough to tie a knot around each small rubber band.

On second thought: Guinevere is a striking style, but it's also a bit time-consuming. For ladies on the run, try Lady Gardenia. Follow steps 1–2, but the ponytails should all have the same thickness and should get only one strand of ribbon each. Braid each ponytail, using the ribbon as the third section, and secure each end with a small rubber band. Take each braid and loop it up, tucking the ends underneath the small rubber bands. Use more ribbon to tie a knot around each rubber band. You should end up with six royal petals.

Spider Girl

With this creepy-crawler creation, black pipe cleaners serve a dual purpose: they allow your braided "spider legs" to bend into web-spinning position, and they give your braids that fuzzy, black spidery look. Although Spider Girl has a lot of steps (no pun intended), it's actually an easy style to do once you get the hang of it.

1. Make a center part from forehead to nape. Use a large hair clip to clip the left section out of the way.

2. On the right side of the head, part the hair again, this time horizontally rather than vertically, so that one section is on top of the other. Use the other large hair clip to clip the top section out of the way (see illustration 1).

3. Make a ridge braid with the bottom section, starting with the hair closest to the face and running toward the back of the head. When there is no more hair to *add,* but still some unbraided, hanging hair, secure with a black elastic.

4. Unclip the top section of hair and make another ridge braid that runs above and parallel to the first braid. Again, secure with a black elastic when there is no more hair to add. Both braids should have "ponytails" sticking out the other side of the elastic (see illustration 2).

5. Take the top "ponytail" and divide it into two sections. Clip one section out of the way.

Spider Girl

6. Slip up to three pipe cleaners underneath the elastic and bend the tips over the elastic so that each pipe cleaner is secured. Braid the remaining section of hair, making sure each pipe cleaner lies neatly on top of each section. Secure the end with a small rubber band. If the pipe cleaners are sticking out of the bottom, trim to size (see illustration 3).

7. Unclip the other section from the top ponytail, and repeat step 6.

8. Repeat steps 5–7 with the bottom ponytail.

9. You should have two ridge braids that split and become four simple "spider leg" braids on the right side of the head (see illustration 4).

10. Repeat steps 2–8 on the left side of the head.

11. When all eight braids are complete, carefully slip a small black scrunchie over each elastic to hide the pipe cleaner tips.

12. Get your spider legs in web-spinning position by folding each one in half.

On second thought: For those who like the attitude but want something less extreme, try Goth Girl. Skip the pipe cleaners, letting the eight braids hang loosely. Then tie long, dangling strands of black velvet ribbon around the elastics, and a black velvet bow at the end of each braid. With a little white powder and dark red lipstick, you'll be the next Wednesday Addams.

3

4

Cleopatra

With all the gold running through these locks, this flashy 'do will turn heads all day. But of course! What else would you expect from a style fit for a queen?

1. Make a center part from forehead to nape.

2. Make two thin flat twists, starting from the crown and ending at the forehead. They should be parallel and centered on top of the head. When you get to the forehead, give each an extra twist and secure with the elastics (see illustration 1).

3. Slip one strand of gold ribbon underneath each elastic.

4. Divide remaining hair from one flat twist into two sections, using the ribbon as the third section to make a braid. Secure with a small rubber band.

5. Repeat step 4 with remaining hair from the second flat twist (see illustration 2).

Accessories

2 elastics

Approximately 20 strands of gold cord-like ribbon

Approximately 40 small rubber bands (clear, if possible)

Bobby pins

Gold beads

Techniques

Flat twist

Simple braid

Braiding in ribbons

Braided coil

Adding beads

Hair length

Any

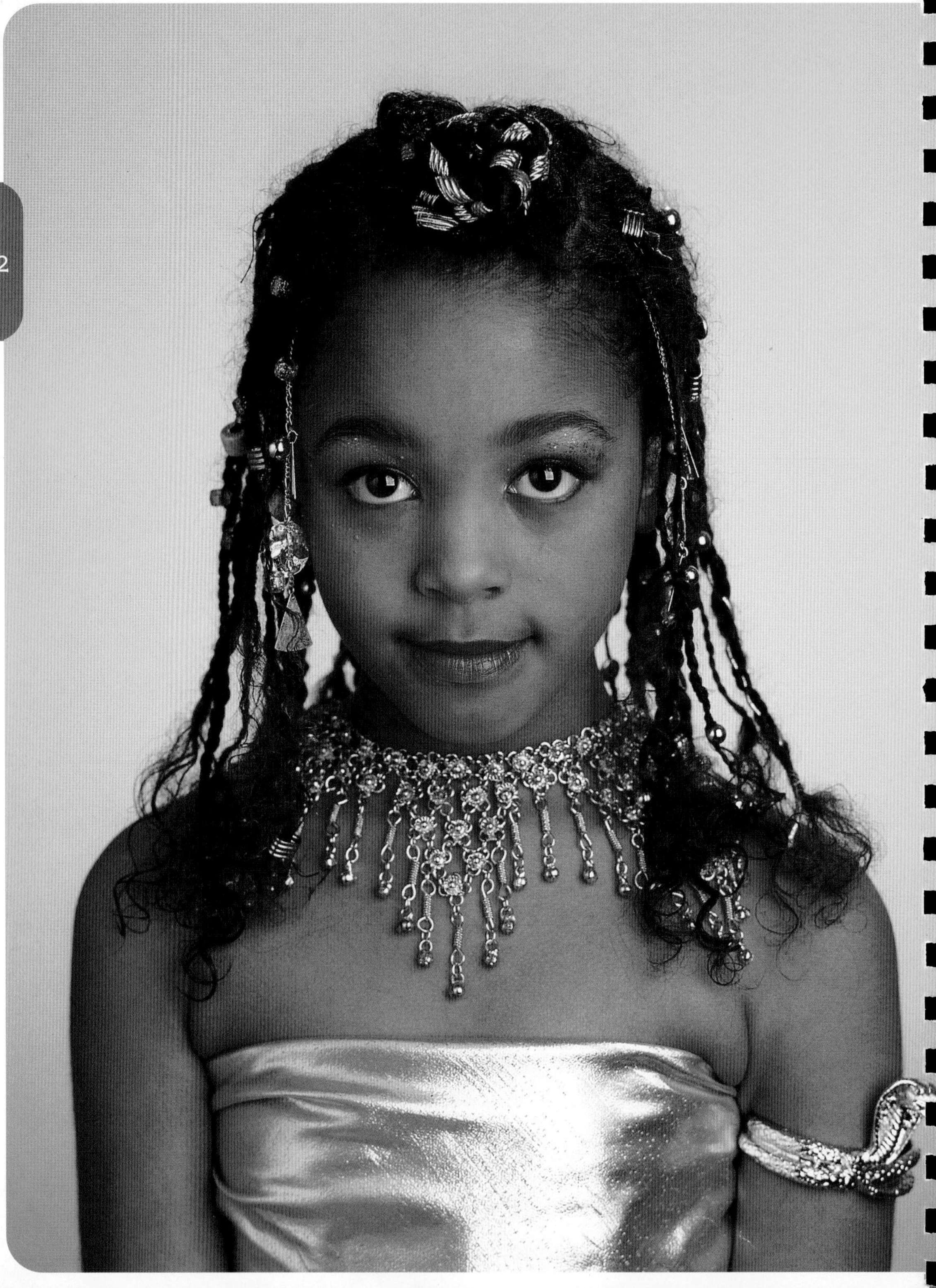

Cleopatra

6. Twist the two braids together until you get to the ends (see illustration 3).

7. Coil these braids, which are now twisted together so that they're like one thicker braid, and position the coil on top and in the center of the forehead. Secure with bobby pins.

8. Make as many thin braids as you can with the rest of the hair, securing the ends with small rubber bands. Start some—or all—of the braids as small ponytails and secure by knotting a strand of gold ribbon around the top of the to-be-braided hair. With these braids, divide hair into two sections, using the gold ribbon as the third section.

9. To make this royal 'do even more regal, add gold beads to some or all of the braids.

On second thought: If you want the Cleopatra look in less than forty minutes, try the Alexandria. Clip aside a thin top layer of hair. With the rest of the hair, make three ponytails on either side of the head and secure with elastics (gold, if possible). Slip three strands of ribbon underneath each elastic and braid each ponytail, making sure each ribbon lies neatly on top of each section. After six braids are made, unclip the top layer of hair and make six to eight small ponytails on each side of the head. Slip one strand of gold ribbon underneath each rubber band and divide each ponytail into two sections, using the ribbon as the third section. Braid each ponytail and secure the ends with small rubber bands. Add gold beads if desired.

3

Sugar Plum Fairy

Although here we've made five purple "plums," you could save time by cutting your crop to only four cornrows and coils. Then pull out your tutu and pirouette over to the Kingdom of Sweets.

1. Make five cornrows, running from the forehead toward the back of the head. You may want to start with the third, or middle, cornrow, which should run across the center of the head, where the center part would normally be. Then add two more cornrows on either side of the middle one.

2. Stop the cornrows when you're still on top of the head and secure with the elastics.

3. Slip one strand of ribbon into each elastic and braid the remaining loose hair from each cornrow, dividing the hair into two sections and using the ribbon as the third section. Secure each braid with a small rubber band (see illustration).

4. Coil each braid, making sure the ribbon faces outward, so that it shows. Secure the coils with bobby pins.

5. If desired, clip some hair jewels along the cornrows before spreading your wings and fluttering away.

On second thought: Feeling more footloose and fancy free? Do only steps 1–3, using elastics with colorful plastic balls, and an Arabian Dancer you shall be.

Accessories

5 elastics

5 strands of thin ribbon

5 small rubber bands

Bobby pins

Optional: clip-on hair jewels

Techniques

Cornrows

Braiding in ribbons

Braided coil

Hair length

Any

Acknowledgments

My biggest thanks go to my daughter and patient model, Sarina, and to my husband, Mark, who, after witnessing one too many crazy hairstyles on Sarina, suggested I write a braid book.

Hearty thanks also go to everyone who helped me put this book together: My editor, Mikyla Bruder; designer, Kristen Nobles; agent, Dan Mandel; illustrator (and hubby), Mark Frauenfelder; photographer, Susan Sheridan (who was also my hand-holding coproducer); stylist, Donna Aira (who taught me the meaning of a wardrobe); makeup and hair stylist, Maria-Elena Arroy; hair stylist, Lynn Tully; makeup assistants, Nedra Hainey and Jenny Yu; lighting kahuna, Sigthor Markusson; supreme production assistants, A. J. D'Agostino and Lynn Aime; and my wonderful models, Sophia Aira, Hannah Bradley, Shannon Crow, Sarina Frauenfelder, Ally and Glenna Gasparian, Karyna Herrera, Allyson Langford, Erica Langford, McKen-Z Leong, Nicole Nagy, Natasha Sheridan, Sophie Sheridan, Rachel Sherman, Olivia Skill, Jodie Lyn Smith, Caroline Weaver, and Hannah Wood.

And a final thank you to Jackie Bly, Melissa and Grant Conway, Bellary Davis, Rebecca and Melissa Feldman, Holly Gasparian, Sheila Jacob, David Pescovitz, Alan Rapp, and Kelly Sparks (who helped with the title).

Carla Sinclair is an author and freelance journalist. She lives in Los Angeles with her husband, daughter, and lovebird.

Susan Sheridan is a photographer whose work has appeared in magazines, newspapers, and TV commercials. Originally from London, England, she now lives in Los Angeles with her husband and two daughters.

Mark Frauenfelder is a freelance journalist, and the illustrator and author of *Mad Professor,* published by Chronicle Books. He lives in Los Angeles with his daughter and wife, Carla, the author of this book.